Tony Romo

by Michael Sandler

Consultant: Norries Wilson
Head Football Coach
Columbia University

BEARPORT
PUBLISHING

New York, New York

Credits

Cover and Title Page, © Joe Robbins/Getty Images, Jason Pyle/CSM/Landov, and Mike Stone/Reuters/Landov; 4, © Scott Boehm/Getty Images; 5, © G. Newman Lowrance/NFL/Getty Images; 6, © Streeter Lecka/Getty Images; 7, © Jeffery Washington/Fort Worth Star-Telegram/MCT/Newscom; 8, © Jim Sloslarek/Journal Times; 9, © Jim Slosiarek/Journal Times; 10, © Eastern Illinois/Collegiate Images/Getty Images; 11, © Icon SMI; 12, © Tom Berg/NFL/Getty Images; 13, © Donna McWilliam/AP Photo; 14, © James D. Smith/Icon SMI; 15, © Icon SMI; 16, © John Pyle/CSM/Newscom; 17, © Scott Anderson/Journal Times; 18, Courtesy of The Wettengel Family; 19, Courtesy of The Wettengel Family; 20, © Ian Halperin/UPI/Landov; 21, © Eric Schlegel/Dallas Morning News/Corbis; 22L, © Newscom; 22R, © Vern Verna/Ai Wire/Landov.

Publisher: Kenn Goin
Senior Editor: Lisa Wiseman
Creative Director: Spencer Brinker
Photo Researcher: Jennifer Bright
Design: Dawn Beard Creative

Library of Congress Cataloging-in-Publication Data

Sandler, Michael.
  Tony Romo / by Michael Sandler ; consultant, Norries Wilson.
    p. cm. — (Football heroes making a difference)
  Includes bibliographical references and index.
  ISBN-13: 978-1-936087-60-0 (library binding)
  ISBN-10: 1-936087-60-X (library binding)
  1. Romo, Tony, 1980- 2. Football heroes—United States—Biography. I. Title.
  GV939.R633S26 2010
  796.332092—dc22
  [B]

               2009031216

For more information, write to Bearport Publishing Company, Inc., 45 West 21st Street, Suite 3B, New York, New York 10010. Printed in the United States of America.

10 9 8 7 6 5 4

CONTENTS

Tony's Big Chance

"Romo, you're in!"

Tony Romo had been waiting three years to hear these words. The Dallas Cowboys quarterback was a **backup**. He usually only played in practice. Now, at halftime against the New York Giants in 2006, his coach was calling his name.

Tony had a full half to prove he belonged in the NFL. How did he do? Terribly! Over and over, he threw bad passes. The Giants **intercepted** three of them, and the Cowboys lost.

Afterward, Tony was crushed. He'd let his teammates down. He'd blown his big chance! Would Dallas coach Bill Parcells give him another try?

Tony warming up on the sidelines before the game against the Giants on October 23, 2006

Tony attempts to make a pass against the New York Giants.

Tony entered the NFL in the fall of 2003. As a backup, he didn't throw a single regular-season pass during his first three years in the league.

Surprise Starter

Tony couldn't believe it. Coach Parcells did give him another chance. He started at quarterback during the very next game, which was against the Carolina Panthers. It was the first start of Tony's career.

This time, Tony made the most of it. After the Panthers jumped out to a 14-0 lead, Tony brought the Cowboys back. He stayed away from the other team's **defenders** and threw short, crisp, **accurate** passes. By the fourth quarter, Dallas had closed the gap to 14-10.

Then, with Tony leading the way, Dallas exploded with 25 fourth-quarter points. The young quarterback helped his team to an amazing 35-14 victory!

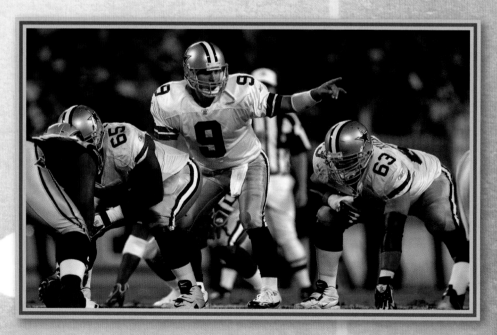

Tony (#9) calls a play to his team during the game against the Panthers.

Tony (#9) scrambles down the field away from the Panthers' defenders.

Dallas's 25-point fourth quarter was a new team record.

Football Latecomer

As a kid growing up in Burlington, Wisconsin, Tony loved playing basketball. In fact, until high school, he rarely played football. Then, as a **freshman**, he decided to join the football team. He did so mainly to keep in shape for basketball. He discovered, however, that he really liked the sport—especially throwing the ball. During his junior year, he became the starting quarterback, racking up yards and leading his team to wins.

Despite his success, Tony didn't attract much attention from **recruiters** at big college football schools. After his senior year, he decided to attend Eastern Illinois University, which only had a **Division 1-AA** program.

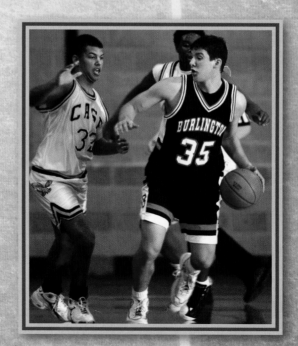

Tony (#35) playing basketball for Burlington High School

Tony threw for 42 touchdowns and nearly 4,000 yards (3,658 m) in two seasons as Burlington High's starting quarterback.

At Burlington High School, Tony played three sports: football, basketball, and golf.

Moving Up

As a Division 1-AA school, Eastern Illinois didn't play the best college football teams. Still, the change from high school was a shock for Tony. College players were bigger, stronger, and tougher than high school players. The coaches were more demanding, too. Tony realized he'd have to work hard to become a better player.

He practiced throwing the football morning, noon, and night. He studied NFL quarterbacks such as Brett Favre and John Elway on TV. He watched how they threw the ball and the way they moved their feet. He tried to copy their moves.

Tony never gave up. All his effort and hard work paid off. By sophomore year, Tony had earned the starter's job.

"I threw the ball so much that there was no way not to improve," said Tony. "I threw six days a week, lots of hours a day, the whole year. I never stopped."

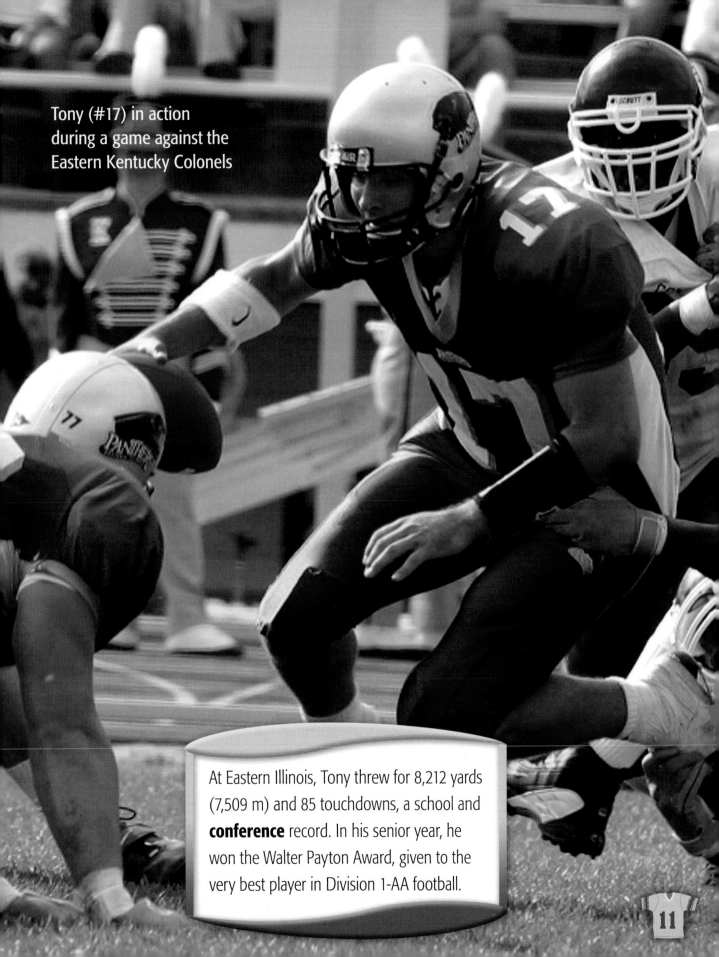

Tony (#17) in action during a game against the Eastern Kentucky Colonels

At Eastern Illinois, Tony threw for 8,212 yards (7,509 m) and 85 touchdowns, a school and **conference** record. In his senior year, he won the Walter Payton Award, given to the very best player in Division 1-AA football.

Not Drafted

Despite Tony's success in college, none of the NFL teams chose him in the 2003 **draft**. Most professional teams weren't very interested in players from Division 1-AA schools. They rarely became NFL stars. The Dallas Cowboys, however, had their eye on the Eastern Illinois college quarterback. They invited him to **training camp** and gave him a chance to make the team.

Surprisingly, Tony made the team, but he didn't get a chance to play. Dallas had other more experienced quarterbacks. They kept Tony around in case these other quarterbacks got hurt.

Tony waited and waited, hoping for a chance. Every day in practice, he worked just as hard as he had in college.

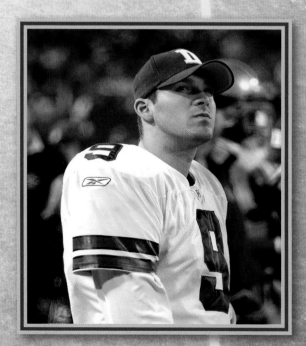

From the sidelines, Tony watches his team play.

Tony (# 9) along with the other Dallas quarterbacks during a practice in 2003

Most NFL teams keep several quarterbacks on their **rosters**.

Success at Last

When Tony got his first start in the big 2006 win over Carolina, many fans were surprised. People didn't expect a backup player to be so good. However, from the moment Tony became the starter, Dallas seemed unable to lose. The Cowboys went 5-1 in his first six starts. Tony completed nearly 70 percent of his passes. He threw one touchdown after another.

After the season ended, Tony was selected to the **Pro Bowl**. Somehow, the longtime backup from Eastern Illinois University had become one of the NFL's very best quarterbacks.

Squirming away from defenders is one of the things Tony does well.

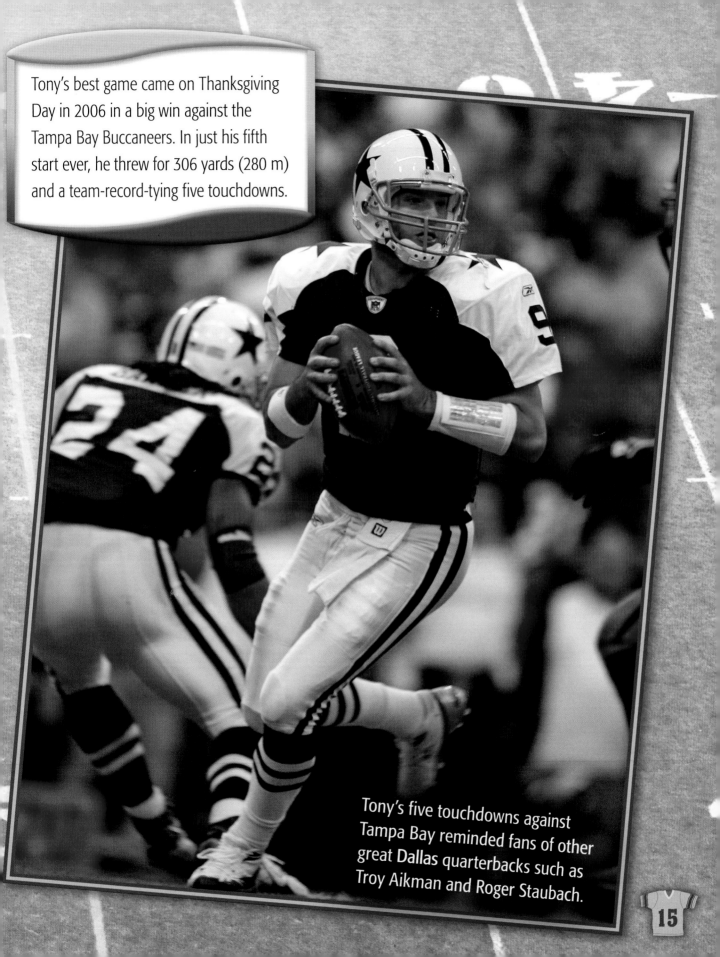

Tony's best game came on Thanksgiving Day in 2006 in a big win against the Tampa Bay Buccaneers. In just his fifth start ever, he threw for 306 yards (280 m) and a team-record-tying five touchdowns.

Tony's five touchdowns against Tampa Bay reminded fans of other great **Dallas** quarterbacks such as Troy Aikman and Roger Staubach.

Receiving and Giving

Hard work, an accurate arm, and a special feel for the game all helped Tony become successful. Help from others also played a big part. As a latecomer to football, he couldn't have developed into such a strong player without lots of great coaching in high school and college.

That's why Tony makes it his business to help others whenever he can. In 2007, for example, he gave $100,000 to Eastern Illinois University. Most of the money went to help the school's sports department.

Tony gives time as well as money. Each summer, he returns to Burlington High to run a football camp for kids. The young athletes—children in the third grade and up—learn football **fundamentals** from Tony himself.

Tony (right) working with some of the Dallas Cowboys' coaches during training camp in 2008

Tony helps a young athlete with his throwing during the Tony Romo Football Camp.

The athletic director of Eastern Illinois University said that Tony's **donation** was one of the largest the department had ever received.

Granting Wishes

Another way Tony helps others is by working with the Make-A-Wish **Foundation**. This group grants special wishes to kids with life-threatening medical conditions.

One of those kids is Paul, a New Jersey nine-year-old who suffers from Primary Ciliary Dyskinesia (PCD). In December 2007, Paul found out he was granted a wish. He knew right away what he wanted. "I wish to meet Tony Romo," he said.

Paul, a lifelong Dallas fan, loved how Tony had brought success to the team. Soon Paul was flying to Dallas to meet his hero and watch him in person at a Cowboys game.

Paul (left) and his brother, Patrick (right), also got a tour of the Dallas locker room and an up-close view of Tony during a practice.

Paul called his Dallas visit to see Tony "the best trip of my life."

PCD is a rare disorder that affects a person's **respiratory system**. It causes frequent lung, ear, and sinus infections.

Big Plans

During Tony's second season as a starter, in 2007, he helped Dallas to an amazing 13-3 record and a run into the playoffs. The following season was tougher. Injuries kept Tony out of key games, and Dallas missed the playoffs.

Still, with Tony as quarterback, Dallas is one of the NFL's top teams. The surprise starter-turned-star is only getting better and better.

Tony dreams of leading Dallas to a Super Bowl. It's not his only goal, though. He wants to start a foundation to help kids improve their lives. "If I can help kids discover what they want to do with their lives and show them how to go about achieving their dreams," said Tony, "that would be the most rewarding kind of work."

Tony (#9) tries to get away from Michael Strahan of the New York Giants during the 2007–2008 NFL playoffs.

Tony signs autographs for his fans.

In only three seasons as a starter, Tony has already broken the Cowboys' record for number of games with more than 300 yards (274 m) passing. Tony has done it 16 times, three more than the previous record holder, Troy Aikman.

The Tony File

Tony is a football hero on and off the field. Here are some highlights.

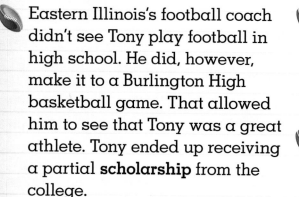

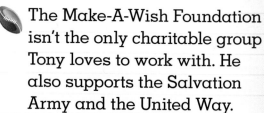

Eastern Illinois's football coach didn't see Tony play football in high school. He did, however, make it to a Burlington High basketball game. That allowed him to see that Tony was a great athlete. Tony ended up receiving a partial **scholarship** from the college.

Tony Romo, a big fan of Tiger Woods, loves golf almost as much as football. He plays whenever he can. He's even tried to qualify for the U.S. Open, a big pro golf tournament.

The Make-A-Wish Foundation isn't the only charitable group Tony loves to work with. He also supports the Salvation Army and the United Way.

When Tony's father, Ramiro, was diagnosed with cancer in 2007, Tony was deeply shaken. Since then, he has thrown himself into the fight against the disease. He appears with his father at events to help raise money to find cancer cures and treatments.

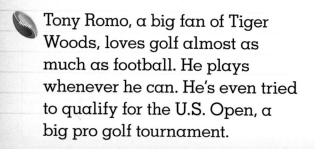

Glossary

accurate (AK-yuh-ruht) precise, on target

backup (BAK-uhp) a player who doesn't start the game and often doesn't play at all

conference (KON-fur-uhnss) a group of college teams that compete against one another

defenders (di-FEND-urz) players who have the job of stopping the other team from scoring

Division 1-AA (di-VIZH-unh WUHN-AYE-AYE) a group of colleges with football teams that do not play at college sports' highest level

donation (doh-NAY-shuhn) a gift of money that is given to help a good cause

draft (DRAFT) an event in which professional teams take turns choosing college players to play for them

foundation (foun-DAY-shuhn) an organization that supports or gives money to worthwhile causes

freshman (FRESH-muhn) a person in his or her first year of high school or college

fundamentals (fuhn-duh-MEN-tuhlz) the basics

intercepted (*in*-tur-SEP-tid) caught by a player on the other team

Pro Bowl (PROH BOHL) the yearly all-star game for the season's best NFL players

recruiters (ri-KROOT-urz) people who have the job of persuading high school players to attend the colleges they represent and play for the college's sports teams

respiratory system (RESS-pi-ruh-*taw*-ree SISS-tuhm) the group of organs in a person's body that helps him or her breathe

rosters (ROS-turz) lists of athletes who make up the players on teams

scholarship (SKOL-ur-ship) an award that helps pay for a person to go to college

training camp (TRANE-ing KAMP) the place where NFL players practice for several weeks as they get ready for a new season

Bibliography

D'Amato, Gary. "Burlington's Boy, Dallas' Hero." *Wisconsin Journal Sentinel* (December 10, 2006).

Layden, Tim. "Silver Star." *Sports Illustrated* (December 11, 2006).

Townsend, Brad. "Favorite Son: Hometown Cheers Romo's Rise." *The Dallas Morning News* (August 29, 2006).

Star-Telegram (Fort Worth)

nj.wish.org

Read More

Bednar, Chuck. *Tony Romo.* Broomall, PA: Mason Crest (2008).

Caffrey, Scott. *The Story of the Dallas Cowboys.* Mankato, MN: Creative Education (2009).

Sandler, Michael. *Troy Aikman and the Dallas Cowboys: Super Bowl XXVII.* New York: Bearport (2009).

Learn More Online

To learn more about Tony Romo and the Dallas Cowboys, visit
www.bearportpublishing.com/FootballHeroes

Index